Either

Ruby Thomas is an actor and writer born in London. She has had short plays performed at the Old Red Lion, Platform Southwark, the White Bear and Theatre 503. She trained on the Soho Theatre Writers Lab and the Royal Court Theatre Supergroup.

RUBY THOMAS

Either

ff

FABER & FABER

First published in 2019
by Faber and Faber Limited
74–77 Great Russell Street, London WC1B 3DA

First published 2019

Typeset by Country Setting, Kingsdown, Kent CT14 8ES
Printed in England by CPI Group (UK) Ltd, Croydon CR0 4YY

A CIP record for this book
is available from the British Library

ISBN 978-0-571-35633-1

2 4 6 8 10 9 7 5 3 1

For Ros and Colin
dancing like that for forty years.

Acknowledgements

With thanks to Charlotte Bennett and
David Luff at Soho Theatre for their support.
Special thanks to Adam Brace, Rebecca Loudon
and Mel Kenyon, without whom the play
would not be what it is.

Either was first performed at Hampstead Theatre
Downstairs on 19 September 2019. The cast, in
alphabetical order, was as follows:

Gabriel Akuwudike
Patrick Knowles
Isabella Laughland
Bianca Stephens
Lizzy Watts
Tilda Wickham

Director Guy Jones
Designer Bethany Wells
Lighting Jamie Platt
Sound Jon McLeod
Movement Rachael Nanyonjo

Characters

The play is written about one couple

A

B

It can be performed by any actors of any genders. The play should be performed with a cast of no less than four actors of various genders and races, who swap in and out of the main two roles and form the ensemble.

Speaking roles in the ensemble are

Cleaner (C)

Passenger (P)

Danny (D)

Therapist (T)

Nurse (N)

EITHER

AUTHOR'S NOTES

The interludes are written to be performed by the ensemble. They can be performed in any order. They can be performed at other times during the play (in between scenes, for example) but they should reach their peak between Scenes Eight and Nine.

*An asterisk * indicates a moment when the cast could switch roles. These can be altered or added as the company sees fit.*

A forward slash / indicates where a character interrupts someone who is already speaking with the following line.

An ellipsis . . . indicates a line where someone intends to speak but can't find the words.

A blank space in place of a printed line indicates a beat of silence.

A line with a dash at the end indicates that the speaker either trails off or is interrupted.

SCENE ONE

At a Pride march. A and B have just bumped into each other. Coffee has been spilt, mainly down A.

B   Fuck.

A   It's fine.

B   I'm so / sorry –

A   Shouldn't drink Starbucks anyway.

B   No.

A   Those lids wash up on the coast of Brazil.

B   Are you –

A   And they don't pay their taxes.

B   Do you need a –

A   And they can't spell anyone's names.

B   Here hold this. I might have a –

   B gives A the cup and looks for a tissue.

A   There's an independent place across the road.

B   That place smells weird.

A   It's just Greek.

B   Here.

   B hands A a tissue.

A   Thanks.

B   Sorry. Shouldn't walk along on my phone.

A   No.

B   I wasn't concentrating –

A   It's fine.

B   Then I looked up and was like, it's you.

A   Me?

B   It's been what? Ten years?
More probably.

A   Probably.

B   How are your parents?

A   OK.
Yours?

B   Divorced. When I was twenty. Pretty sure they were just waiting for us to leave home.

A   Sorry to hear that.

A starts examining the Starbucks cup.

B   Don't be, they're loving life. Mum's got a time-share in Spain. Dad's started wearing a necklace.
This is so weird.
After you moved I tried to –
Sorry, what are you doing?

A   What?
Nothing. Just / looking at –

B   Are you trying to check my name?

A   No.

B   You don't remember my name / do you?

A   Of course I / remember –

B   We lived opposite each other for what?

4

A   Like –

B   A decade?
I'm Ally's mate.
We used to hang out?
On the allotments?

A   The allotments.

B   Yeh.

A   Oh.

B   Yeh.

A   Fuck.

B   So?
What's my name?

A   Um. It's

Uh

It's

E
El?

B   That says extra hot.

A   . . .

B   And below that there's a smiley face.

A   Corporate bullshit.

B   At least it's corporate bullshit with a smile.

A   Sorry.

B   It's fine. Been a while.
We've got spare shirts in my office if you / want to –

A   You're in the office on a Saturday?

B Yeh.

A Where do you work?

B That building right there.

A The one that looks like a fly fucked a prison?

B Yeh.
Wow it really does.

A So you're in –
Business?

B Branding. I do rebranding for companies that –
Whatever it's boring.

A No it's not.

B You're right I don't think the job is boring. I think
I'm boring.
They have a chef and you can bring your dog to
work / so –

A You've got a dog?

B No.
I've always wanted one but –
Committing to an actual dog, with a face, looking up
at me. It's too scary.

A Yeh dogs without faces are much more reassuring.

B I just. Came straight out of uni, got this job.
Don't know who I'd be without it.

A Do you enjoy it?

B Um

Shit that's weird. I have no idea.

A   Anyway, I should probably get back.

B   Yeh. Course.

A   Just nipped off for a piss.

B   Where from?

A   The march.

B   Oh. What is that? Environmental stuff or –

A   The march?

B   Yeh.

A   What is it?

B   . . .

A   It's Pride.

B   Oh.

A   Are you joking? You didn't know it was Pride? There's gay people, everywhere.

B   It is Soho.

A   What did you think that guy was doing? Going for a walk?

B   He's got a leash.

A   Right.

B   Guess I'm not really big on the whole –

Marching thing.

A   Why don't you join? I can spare a flag.

B   I should really.

You're welcome to come up and change.

A   It's fine. Don't mind a bit of mess.
       I'll just take my top off.

B   On second thoughts where can I join?

A   . . .

B   Sorry. I need to get better at –
       Talking.
       You do look

       Do you, work out, or?

A   I'm a carpenter so / that keeps you in shape.

B   A carpenter
       Wow. That's so hip.

       And medieval.

A   Well –

B   Sorry / I didn't mean that to sound –

A   It's not supposed to be hip / it's just a passion I guess.

B   Sorry, you go –

A   My dad taught me to whittle when I was a kid.

       A hands B a business card.

       All my stuff is recycled. Made to measure. These
       cards used to be coffee cups.

B   'Chrysalis Carpentry'.

A   If you ever need any office furniture.

B   I think we just bulk buy Ikea.

A   Well. Nice seeing you. Good luck with / the whole –

B   Can we just talk a bit longer?

Sorry.
Been staring at a screen all day.
I work most weekends.
Then I go to the gym.
But my gym's next door to KFC and I think I'm
addicted to Zinger burgers.
And I have this weird thing where when I'm drunk
I order stuff off Amazon and then three days later
I get a package and it's like –
A book on space?

A They don't pay their taxes either.

B In space?

A Amazon.

B Yesterday I tried to walk down an up escalator
because I was playing Minesweeper on my phone.
I'm that person.

A Minesweeper? Wow.

B I've forgotten my password for the app store.

A . . .

B I don't know why I'm telling you all this.
I just came out of a long relationship so –
Think I'm just having an identity crisis.

*

A Oh, I'm sorry.
Was it serious?

B Nine years.

A Fuck.

B By the end it felt more like a life sentence. Just with
less sex in the shower.

A Funny.

B Thought of it in the shower yesterday, just waiting to try it out.

A Yeh, you need to get out more.

B I would love to.
With you.
I mean. Go for a drink. Or a coffee. Proper coffee.
Somewhere in Hackney with –
A book exchange. And oat milk.

A OK.

B I've only got my work phone on me but –
Are you on Facebook?

A No.
I guess it's now or never.

A holds out a rainbow flag.

Go on, take it.
I've got whistles and face-paint too.

*

SCENE TWO

At a wedding.

A When did Ally get posh?

B Everyone gets like this about weddings. They think they won't but –

A . . .

B My ex Sam wanted to get married, said we'd have to save up thirty grand.

A Thirty? For what?

There's a tree over there we're meant to hang messages on. I want to write one saying, how many trees did you have to kill to make these pointless fucking messages?

B I thought the place-name things were sweets. Ate mine. Turns out, they are pebbles.

A Pebbles.

B That's my next pay cheque down the drain on the dentist.

A Oh well. They're usually fit and South African right?

B Where did you meet white boots?

A My date?

B Mm.

A My date's name is Jo.

B Nice.

And just to check, those are actually white boots? To a wedding?

A I like them.

B Sure, just don't look directly at them. What are they made of, the moon?

A Alright.

B How did you meet Jo?

A At a rave.

B No.

You met someone / at a rave.

A In Epping Forest. Few weeks back.

B A few weeks?
Are you

Together?

A Nah. Just can't resist a plus one.

B What, like a coupon? Buy one get one free?

A No. Coupons are a marketing ploy to make you buy things you don't want.

B I know that. I work in branding.

A Oh yeh.

B That's how it works, we just want stuff, and stuff, and stuff. The quality becomes less important than the adrenaline of buying a new thing.

A Bit depressing.

B I'm on Tinder, of course I'm depressed.
It's like canapés. No one actually wants the canapé, they just want something to cover up life's awkwardness. Keep your hands busy.

A Masticate.

B . . .

A It means chew.

B Sure.

A That how you met Sam? Tinder?

B No. We met on a night out at college.

A   See? A night out.

B   Yeh but. An acid rave.

A   No one calls them that.
    Loser.

B   I am a loser.
    I blame my parents.

A   Whenever I picture them, I think of one of those
    wooden trees you hang mugs on.

B   Pretty accurate.
    Yours were so cool. In number twelve, with the
    hanging plants.
    They let you get that blond strip in your hair that
    turned green in the lido.

A   Yeh.

B   They seemed so in love.

A   Still are.

B   You still close to them?

A   Yeh.
    My dad's not very well so –

B   Oh, I'm sorry.

    Is it –

A   Do you want to dance?

B   Me? No.

A   Why not?

B   People might see.

A   Who cares?

B   I look like a dick.

A   Now I really want to dance.

B   I don't have rhythm.

A   Make it up.
       Come on. Don't be / boring.

B   Fine. Fine.
       OK.
       OK.

       They dance together.
       It starts off awkward, then gets more fun.

A   See?

       They get closer together.
       Then further apart.

*

       Then closer together.

       When was the last time we / even –

B   Years ago. On the allotment.

A   No, I meant, saw each other. Not –

B   Oh –

A   Christ.

B   I thought you meant –
       Fuck.

A   It's OK.

B   Sorry.
       It was at Pride.

A   Right.

B   . . .

A Don't stop.

A keeps dancing with B.

A The allotments.
Think about them a lot, do you?

B Some of the stuff we did by those tomato plants was
definitely –

Formative.

A Really?

B You never knew when Alan was going to pop up
with his trowel.

A Alan.
I forgot Alan.

B He was part of one of those community groups
wasn't he? For

People with –

A Mental health. Just say mental health.

B We took those Polaroids.

A Shit.

B Wonder what happened to them.

A Dread to think.

B indicates a couple dancing nearby.

B How long do you think they've been dancing like
that?

A Thirty years?

B You don't find that at a rave.

A Or on Tinder.

B   Or anywhere really.

A   Not often.

They stop dancing.

B   Think those canapés / might be a bit dodgy, my
stomach's –

A   Why don't you buy Jo a ticket?

B   Sorry. You go.

A   I said. Why don't you buy Jo a train ticket? Home.

B   Huh?

A   You said you wanted to take me out, that time / at
Pride.

B   I know that's shit, I should have called –

A   That's OK.

B   Just seemed a bit
Random.

A   Life is random.

B   And you gave me a card. I mean, who has cards?
Where do you put them?

A   I'm just saying. We're here now. Let's do it.

B   But. Jo –

A   Jo doesn't care.
Jo's a liberal.

B   Liberals have feelings.
Last I checked they have a lot of them.

A   Jo came to a stranger's wedding in white boots. Jo's
laid back.

B . . .

A Ah you know what, look, it doesn't matter. It was /
just an idea –

B No, wait a minute.

A I'll stick with Jo. Maybe we'll bump into each other
again / some other –

B Well hang on. You came on the train, did you?

A Yeh.

B I've got a car.

A You could drive me home in the morning.

B Do they have rooms here?

A Apparently we're near Rudyard Kipling's house
so they're named after his stories. Leopard's Spots,
Camel's Hump.

B This is all a joke, isn't it? You're joking.

A No.

B But Jo.

A Jo's just here for the shit Bellinis.

B We do keep meeting.

A We do.

B Like fate.

A No such thing. But sure.

B You don't believe in fate?

A Free will all the way. If I didn't believe in that I'd kill
myself.

B Surely you / believe in –

A Love is just sex. And sex is just chance. And chance is just timing. And free will.
Come on.
It beats swiping, right.

B Less chance of repetitive strain injury.

A I can't promise that.

B . . .

A . . .

B Well

Be my first time since the break up. Ten years same person.

A I'm going to make you come so hard you won't remember your name.

B OK.

A OK?

B OK.

A Good.

B What the fuck do we tell Jo?

A I'll do it.

B What?

A I'll just make something up.

B Let me.

A Seriously?

B Yeh I want to. I'll say –

Southern Trains have an electrical fault, they need someone to light the way with their boots.

A Are you sure?

B Jo's fine. Jo's a raver. Free love, man.

A A raver, not a dickhead.

B Same thing.

A does a face.

A So you're going to handle Jo?

B I'm going to handle Jo.

A I'll get us a room.

B Can't believe we're doing this –

A Good luck.
I'ma take some canapés for sustenance.

B (*flirty*) Why don't you just masticate?

A Yeh, you've totally misunderstood what that means.

SCENE THREE

On the South Bank.

A Something exciting.

B Why?

A It's your birthday. We have to do something you've always wanted to try but never got round to.

B Like?

A I don't know

Take acid?

Fly to Iceland?
Go on the London Eye?
OK, that last one's a bit shit / but you get what –

B Um the London Eye is amazing. Look at it.

A . . .

I'm looking.

B It's beautiful.

A It's a tourist trap. A big machine. Churning around.

B It can still be beautiful just because it's a machine.

A I prefer natural beauty.

B I'll have you know this – (*Points at themself.*) takes a lot to maintain.

A gives B a shove.

B OK OK. Well, I can't do acid. I just know my brain would get stuck and I'd end up

Licking the wallpaper or something.
And I've been to Iceland. All I could think about in the blue lagoon was verrucas.

A Fine. You choose. We've got all afternoon.

B I've never done Laser Quest?

A No.

B What's wrong with / Laser Quest?

A Just no.

B What?

A You're going to die alone if Laser Quest is your first answer.

B Why?

A I don't have to explain, just / say something else –

B OK.
OK.

I'd like to learn to sew.

A . . .

B No seriously, I saw this thing online. It said 'bitch' but in embroidery. On a little thing –

A That's the kind of person you want to become. Someone who makes humorous-abuse embroidery?

B I don't want to become anything, I just want to try some crafts.

A Next.

B Fine.
I've never got a tattoo.

A OK.

And you want one?

B I've always sort of
Wondered.
How do you decide?

A Well what do you want?

B I don't know.

A Can be vague.

B Something that means something.

A Little too vague.

B How did you choose yours?

A I don't know. Just a
Feeling. In the moment, I guess.
This one reminds me of being a teenager, drinking
Smirnoff behind the Odeon.

B The dream.

A I got it with Ally.

B Where was I?

A I don't know. Learning to play the recorder
somewhere.

B . . .

A I like looking at that one. Reminds me of that age,
you know, when every decision mattered both so
much more and so much less.

B Mm.

A This one my friend did. That was about freedom,
making your own path.
That makes me happy because I'll never be as much
of a dick as I was at twenty.

B Thank fuck.
And the other one?

A The other one was for a bet.

B It really is / *very* bad.

A I know I know.

B It's wonky.

A I know it's bad. I got it in Thailand. Think the
tattooist went rogue with a biro and needle.
So come on. What are you feeling right / now?

B I don't know. I feel

Excited?

A Great.

B I feel
Calmer than I have in a long time?
Kind of nostalgic?
But for the present. Like I'm living a past that I'll
enjoy looking back on. Does that make sense?

A Profound.

B Not in a wanky way.

A In a wanky way.

B It's like, I can feel myself changing. In a way I haven't
since, adolescence maybe.

*

But the catalyst is you instead of like, overactive
glands.

A Shall we get one?

B A tattoo?
Now?

A Yeh.

B Of what?

A Anything. We can choose one from their book.

B We?

A You.

B You have to do it too.

A No.

B   It was your idea.

A   That's two in two years. I have a rule where I wait /
    at least –

B   Nah nah nah, don't try and be rational about this.

A   Fine.
    I've had a design in mind for a while. Two lines.
    Simple. So when people ask what it means we can
    make some shit up.

B   Matching tattoos?

A   Why not?

B   It's been six weeks.

A   Who cares?

B   But what if we, you know –

A   Who cares?

B   I saw this guy online who got a picture of his
    girlfriend's face tattooed on his chest, like right there.
    Then they broke up.

A   Won't be of my face though, will it?

B   I mean, imagine being his next girlfriend.

A   It'll remind you of being in love. It doesn't matter
    who / it was.

B   Love?

A   . . .

B   You said it.

A   Slip of the tongue.

B   Freudian.

A I said you love me not I love you.

B Well, I don't.

A That's fine then.

B I don't love you.

A Then it won't matter / will it, so that's fine.

B I honestly don't love you, I just want to be clear about that.

A So do it.

B Are you bullying me?

A No.

B This is just like the allotment.

A You were the one who said you feel like you're disappearing.
Tattoos are like the real-life version of pinching yourself so you wake up.

B Bit more permanent.

A Nothing's really permanent though, is it? We'll all be gone in eighty years.

B Happy birthday.

A Look up the nearest tattoo parlour.
And I'll draw it on so you can see.

Where do you want it?

B On my arm.

A Here?
Ready?

B I think so.

A Here we go.

A draws on B.

A How does that feel?

B Well fine, but that's a ballpoint.

B looks at their phone.

The nearest place is 1.4 miles away. G. Dawson says 'Sik job, I look propa gangsta.'

A Sounds right up your alley.

B Fuck it, let's get shots on the way.

SCENE FOUR

In a supermarket. B is carrying a basket.

B It's neither.

A It's neither.

B No, neither is American.

A It's subjective.

B No, the Americans are wrong.
Can you carry the basket or what is the point of you?

A takes the basket.

B I'm just saying 'neither' is an Americanism.

Like

Yoghurt. Or Adidas.

A No one says Adidas.

B OK fine. Nike.

A I say Nike.

B No you don't.

A Sometimes I do.

B I've heard you say Nike.

A Like to keep it fresh.

B Do it for me then. 'Neither' is just one of my words.

Like

Moist.

Or pussy.

A I love pussy.

B . . .

A I'm just saying no words are wrong. Why rule them out. We should be / open to –

B What about the N word?

A It's made a comeback.

B Not for everyone. Not everyone can use it. We're a case in point.

A So PC.

B I hate it when people say PC like it's a bad thing. PC just means being nice. I'm nice.

A makes a face.

A I'm just saying, words are just words. Why label them?

B This is tiring.

A Poor baby's got a hangover. Let's get some eggs.

B No, it's tiring you acting like you're cleverer than me all the time.

A ?

B   You're smug. You know that.

A   I'm –

B   You're one of those smug people.

A   Those people?

B   You pretend you're open-minded but you never just let me have an opinion.

A   I let you have opinions.
     I just don't agree with them.

B   You make me feel stupid.

A   Come on –

B   Like with that film.

A   You kept asking me who he was. We're watching the same film. It's ten minutes in. He looks a bit like Vin Diesel, that's all I've got.

B   I might have missed something.
     It was so dark.

A   It was Danish.

B   It was a minefield.

A   If you weren't on your phone all the time.

B   . . .

A   Even during sex.

B   One time. You started before I was ready.

A   I'm down there, doing my thing, and I hear, swoosh. Email sent.

B   One time.

A   Just google an orgasm next time.

B   Fuck off and find some eggs.

A Oh my God.

B What?

A Is this our first fight?

B . . .

A Three months in. That's about right. Isn't it?
    Is it? I don't really do relationships.

B Wonder why.

A And in public. God, that is sexy. In this huge
    corporate shit storm.

B Christ.

A You know if you combine all the primary colours
    you just get brown? So this literally is a shit storm.

B So pretentious.

A We're star-crossed lovers in in in –
    An urban malaise.

    A shopper (S) walks past.

B Shut up.

A Kiss me.

B What's a malaise?

A Who cares.

B Sounds like a condiment.

A It's like, illness or sadness or the shit all around us
    that we don't care about because we're here, arguing
    over your phone.
    Kiss me!

B Please / stop showing off –

A   Come on, kiss me in the home cleaning and pet food aisle. Kiss me or I drink this bleach!

B   Come on / people are starting to –

A   I'm going to drink antifreeze and die and they'll have to put out those yellow cones and an old lady will slip on my guts and she'll die. Kiss me!

B kisses A.

S   Excuse me.

B   Sorry.

S   Thanks.

The shopper goes past them.

A   Welcome to the shit storm.

B   Twat.

A   You love it.

B   You always do this. Make me feel stupid and then turn it into a joke so I have to laugh about it.

A   . . .

B   Seriously. Just because I'm not an 'artist'.
Or a member of the Labour Party.

A   I only do the one-off payment thing for elections. I'm a fraud.

B   I know.

Is this about earlier?

A   What?

B   Your dad.

A   What about him?

B   You always get like this when he rings.

A Like what?

B All hard and distant.

A I'm not distant.

B If you want to talk / about it –

A I'm fine.

B It must be hard when he / forgets things.

A I'm fine. I was just messing.

B Are you sure?

A Yes.

B OK.

Right.

What's next?

A Eggs.

And let's get doughnuts and have pudding at breakfast. Fuck the system.

B Ooh yes. Jam or custard?

A Either.

B . . .

SCENE FIVE

In a public toilet. A and B finish having sex.

B Fuck.

A . . .

B Fuck.

A Yeh.

They both take a few deep breaths.

B Thought someone was going to come in in the middle, did you?

A Mm.

B Quite hot actually.

B kisses A.

B I love looking down and seeing our little tattoos.

A . . .

B I feel like something sweet. Do you feel like something sweet?
Like a doughnut.

B fastens their trousers.

B We should probably get out of here / before –

A Do you like me?

B What?

A . . .

B Of course I like you.

A I mean, really like me?

B Ever since the allotment, baby, you have had pride of place in my wank bank.

Sorry. Endorphins.

A That's the thing

B   What?

A   I think I might really like you –

B   OK.

A   A lot.

B   OK.
Just say it.

A   . . .

B   Say the thing you're scared to say.

A   Scared?

B   You're tiptoeing around it. Just say it. I might even say it back.

A   Fine. I really like you –

B   No, see, you've misunderstood the game.

A   I really like you and it's making me nervous –

B   / Yes.

A   Because I think I still want to sleep with other people.

I do. Really like you.
I do.
I think you're amazing / but –

B   I think we should probably –

B starts to leave.

A   Wait wait wait –

B   No, we are in the Barbican toilets, I don't think this is the time / for a –

A   You brought us in here.

B Because I wanted to do something you've never done before on your birthday, because I know you like that. And now you're what? Breaking up with me?

A No.

B When I've just come? That is dark.

A Please –

B I can still feel you drying on my leg.
In fact, pass me a hand towel.

A Can I say something?

B Well, I suppose better here than in the porno sculpture exhibition you made me go to.

A It's not porn, she's celebrating the body. Pushing the boundaries of the erotic.

B Glad someone managed to.

A I don't want to break up.

B Look it's fine, it's only been six months.

A Six great months.

B Oh fuck.

A What?

B 'Six great months'. That's so
Platitudey. Like 'Thanks for coming in, Justin'.

A Who's Justin?

B 'We can't keep you in the mix at this stage but you've been a great cog in the old machine.'

A OK, I really don't know / what you're talking –

B Just don't give me work-speak. I know about work-speak.

A I don't want to break up. I'm just.
Not done with other people.

B You don't have to be done. You just have to be done
for now.

A Why?

B Because.

A It's like. You know how we both got obsessed with
that Aimee Mann album? And you listened to it
again and again for two weeks and I got annoyed
because I also needed, you know –
Some Antwon.

B Some –

A A bit of throwback Ja Rule.

B What?

A Variety. I need variety.

B You're saying. What? An open relationship?

A Maybe.

B There is a name for that, you know.

A Polyamory?

B Having your cake and eating it.

A Great. Hilarious.
But look. I love you.

B You love me?

A You're my
My only
Proper person. I've never felt like this before.

B So what am I, seventy per cent, you just need the other thirty?

A No –

B What don't I give you?

A You can't get everything from one person.

B But what part of everything am I not good at? The sex? The politics? The haircut?

A Everything doesn't come in parts.

B People do. And then you pick one.

*

A Why do we have to?

B Because that's love. It's not music. It's about compromise.

A That's what they feed you.

B Who?

A The patriarchal agenda.

B Oh for / fuck's sake –

A It's about intimacy. Affection. If you trust someone emotionally what does it matter what they do with their genitals?

B Because –

A It's conditioning.
Based on feudal structures and land ownership and and
I read this book, about this tribe in Brazil, where the women have sex with as many men as they can, so their kid gets all the different attributes.
I mean, obviously that's not
Scientific but –

B   ...

A   This isn't natural.

B   What about your parents?

A   Great. Psychoanalysis.

B   I'm just saying.
     They still kiss with tongues.

A   What about your parents?

     Sorry but –

B   It's fine. My parents got married at twenty-two. They
     didn't know who they were.

A   Exactly.

B   They were happy for almost thirty years. They just
     grew apart.

A   Maybe they didn't have to.

B   Trust me. They did.
     But we still do Christmas together. Their marriage
     wasn't a failure just because –

     I wouldn't exist otherwise.

A   What about you and Sam?

B   ...

A   You got bored, right?
     Why do you think people get bored or have affairs
     or end / up hating each other –

B   Because they're arseholes?

A   Because this isn't normal.

B   Everyone else thinks it's normal.

A   But this tribe in Brazil –

B   Shut the fuck up about Brazil. OK? Don't –
     You can't just drag Brazil into this.

A   Look.
     OK.
     Do you masturbate?

B   What?

A   Hear me out. You do, right?

B   Well.
     Not so much at the moment / but –

A   But sometimes.

B   Of course I masturbate.
     I'm very good at it.

A   OK, well I started when I was nine. Maybe younger.
     I did it all the time, every night. Maybe everyone
     does, I don't know. It's not the kind of thing you can
     ask other kids without getting detention. And when
     I came it felt amazing but it also felt really –

     Unfinished. I remember thinking, how am I ever
     going to use all of this up? It was like it was
     Welling up inside me.

     And as I got older it got even better. I used to love
     that buzz of meeting someone and wanting each
     other and. That moment where taking and giving
     both mean the same thing and you can forget all the
     politics. Because relationships are political, but casual
     sex is not. And I am happy to work out the politics of
     'us' but / I don't want to.

B   I always kind of hated casual sex. Like eating a dry
     cracker because there's nothing else in the cupboard.

A   It's not about that. Consuming for the sake of it.
It's about
Wanting to live
More of life.
You are the person I care about. But there are so
many other people out there who I look at and think
'Wow, what's your story?' Not in a wet, married-
with-kids-but-still-daydreams-on-the-tube way, I
mean I want to go out there and / meet them –

B   Fuck them. Yeh, I got that.

You think I don't want to fuck other people? I do.
I just think the most exciting thing I could do is
choose. Build something. Random
Scrambly sex is the same every time.

*

With you it's different.

A   No one's coming.

B   Is there someone else?

A   What?

B   Some chance encounter? Someone at the workshop?

A   No. I might not even meet anyone, if we –

I just don't want to close that door, hit fifty and
think, life passed me by.

B   I feel like saying the same to you. I'm what's here
now aren't I? This is it.

A   Is it?

B   Just imagine from my perspective. Everything's going
well. I feel better than I have in years. I'm not going
to KFC because you make vegetarianism so fucking

delicious. And now it's like I've been talking to myself the whole time. You're everything I want.

You said you loved me. You said all this shit but you also let slip that you love me. And that's the bit I remember.

So stupid –

A It's not –

B Look just give me some time. OK? There's a lot of Stuff there.

But I'll think about it.

A OK.

Think quick though, I'm going out with Ally on Friday and I need to know whether to shave down there –

B . . .

A It's a joke.

B exits.

A I was joking. I was just trying to lighten the –

A washes their hands.

A Barbican (C) cleaner enters.

A Look, I'm sorry that was really –

A looks up.

Oh. Sorry. I thought you were someone else.

C No.

A   These are unisex toilets, right? I'm not –

C   Yeh. They are. You're fine.

A   OK.
Right.

C   . . .

A   I'll get out of your way, sorry.

C   You're fine.

C starts cleaning.

A stands alone for five to ten seconds.

*

SCENE SIX

In a café. A and B sit together.

A   I've missed you.
Being ignored is ironically really distracting. I haven't been able to think about anything else.

B   What about anyone else?

A   Touché.

Yeh.

Thanks for meeting me?
In a vegan café no less.

B   They do good coffee.

A   Look, I'm really sorry for –
The Barbican, of all places, is way too brutalist for a heart-to-heart.

B Mm.

A These past six weeks

I've been spending a lot of time with Dad.

He forgot my name for the first time the other day. I was there for three hours and he called me the carer's name, the neighbour's name. But not mine.

B I'm sorry.

A It's OK.
Kind of funny watching TV with him. He can't follow plotlines so we just watch that dumb home video show. What's it called?

B *You've Been Framed*.

A Yeh.
He used to be such a snob. Thought David Attenborough was lowbrow.
Kept wishing you were there to laugh about it.

I'll do whatever you need. If you need more time I'll stop the calls. And the voice notes, especially the ones where I sing –

B Didn't get them.

A What?

B The voice notes.

B holds up their phone. It is an old model with a flip top.

A New phone.

B Well. Old.

I quit my job.

A What?

B Had a meeting with my boss. Said I needed a change. Afterwards I was standing outside the Starbucks where we met and I chucked my phone in the bin.

Then I got it out because it's a work phone and I still had three weeks' notice but.
I bought this one because I can stop checking in.
I don't have to be in the loop.

A You quit?

B Yeh.

A I –

Congratulations?

B Thanks.

A Am I allowed to –

B Yeh.

They hug.

B I thought about what you said, about daydreaming on the tube / about other people.

A Sorry, that was –

B No. I'm glad you said it. Because I realised, I'm doing that with my job. Every day, I sit on the tube, or stand, and think.
I essentially work in a prison full of glass cells and men called
Hugo. What am I doing? Being a grown-up? What for? So I applied for a Master's.

A In what?

B History of Art.

A Wow.

That really is the opposite of a sensible job.

B I might have to move, get a bar job, who cares.

A . . .

B Actually it was so funny when I quit because I went out the night before with Ally. Some party in Hackney.

I took MDMA. I mean imagine me on MDMA. It wasn't cute.

And in my exit interview I touched my boss's face, twice.

Think he thought I was coming on to him but

Anyway the point is I'm sorry I got upset. I needed time to –

Well, I felt rejected but. I've thought about it a lot and

When we met I thought you were so exciting. And then I went about doing everything I could to turn you into someone boring.

A Boring?

B Not –

A You don't have to take MDMA to not be boring. In fact it has the opposite effect.

B I just mean I was so desperate for things to be serious. Staying over all the time. Taking you to meet my nan.

A I like your nan.

B She's a bit UKIP.

A Well –

At least she's vintage UKIP. She liked UKIP before it was cool.

B The point is, that was the old me. I let my insecurities get in / the way of –

A Your insecurities?

B That you're better than me. More interesting.

A And now you think I'm not better?

B I think we might both be good.

A Great.

Great.

B How have you been?

A Pretty much sat on the phone singing you voice notes.

B Slept with anyone?

A Honestly?

Yes.
Have you?

B No. But that's OK.
No one you like?

A No one like you.

B How's Chrysalis?

A Good yeh. We got investment.

B Seriously?

A An angel investor I pitched to last month.

B How much?

A Quite a bit.

B Seriously?

A Enough to build the website.

A gets out their phone, which is a new one, to show B.

See? All my designs are in the boxes. You just click to order.

B Nice.

A Hired a guy in the workshop. Now I just run around updating things.

B A well-oiled machine.

Do you want to go back to yours and –

A   I need to work. Later?

B I've got pottery at eight.

A Pottery?

B I've taken up crafts.

A . . .

B Don't judge me and you might get a vase out of it.

A OK.

B Thank you.

A For what?

B I feel like I've turned a corner. Since we met.
   Like starting again.

*

A So what, this is our first date?

B Yeh. And you know what that means? No monogamy. I'm excited.

A Me too.
   Call me after pottery.

B This time I actually will.

In an airport.

A   A girl?

B   A woman.

A   A woman.

Wow.

B   You're not angry are you?

A   No of course not.
I just didn't realise you'd –

No good for you.

B   Where's Gate 28?

A   Just some random woman?

B   I can see 27 and 29.

A   Not someone we know?

B   No, I know the rules. A stranger. I tell them about
you. And I take mental notes of their flaws to tell you
after.

A   That's not a rule.

B   Added that one for my safety.

A   Where did you meet her, on an app?

B   No, don't have a smartphone, do I?

A   Online? Guardian Soulmates? OkCupid? Coffee
Meets Bagel?

B   There's not actually one / called –

A   Trust me. There is.

B   Why don't you just ask someone out in real life?

A   I'm running a business. The last thing I want to do on a Friday is go to a bar and chat up some kid with a top knot.

B   I got someone's number in the supermarket the other day.

A   Another girl?

B   A guy.

A   Jeez.

B   You always say it's a spectrum.

A   Yeh, but pick an end. For ten minutes.

B   Where is Gate 28?

A   Over there by the loos.

B   Well that doesn't make sense. Why do airports make sense until the gates, then it's 9 to 17 that way, except 12 downstairs and 16b in a parallel universe?

A   So where was she from?

B   Pottery.

A   Oh nice, how's her hip replacement?

B   She's in her thirties.

A   Attractive?

B   See, this is where my flaw rule kicks in. She had too many moles and a bump in her nose.

A   But other than that?

B   She was

Pretty.
Don't sit, we need to queue.

A   No one queues. The seats are unallocated.

B   That's why we queue. To get a good one.

A   Boy pretty or girl pretty?

B   What?

A   You're the one who always says there's a difference.

B   Only in branding.

A   Men like lip liner and waist-to-hip ratios. Girls like
Freckly alien babes.

B   Not in real life.

A   Fine but –

B   I don't know. If I asked the people here what they
thought of her and turned it into a pie chart, the pie
would be
Mainly yellow. Or whatever colour pretty was in
this, graph scenario.

A   Let's see a picture.

B   She's not on social media.

A   Ooh –

B   Where are the passports?

A   In the poncey purse thing.
So you're at pottery?

B   We went to the park. People left.
The pottery lot aren't big ravers.

A No.

B So then it was just us. We were chatting –

A You'd told her about me?

B No.

A The rules –

B I know, but I suddenly realised how hard that is. I mean, do you tell them straight away and risk scaring them or do you wait and risk seeming secretive?

A Yeh / OK so –

B So in the end I just waited for a lull and went, monogamy, eh?

A Smooth.

B Worked actually. She went on a rant about how it's patriarchal bullshit. I nodded. Told her about you. Then we kissed.

A She sounds laid back.

B She's Brazilian –

A Oh God

B Well, half Brazilian, half Dutch.

A What the fuck? Is she made up?

B No. It's like you said.

*

B The world is full of interesting people.

A So what, you kissed?

B Then we went back to hers, had a whisky.
And –

A And?

B You really want me to tell you / all the –

A Just give me the quick version.
Like a lethal injection.

B I gave her head, she gave me head, then there was
Penetration.

A How long?

B It was Sunday morning.

A Positions?

B I feel confused about whether / you want –

A Just be general.

B She particularly liked being on top of me.

On my face.

A See, that's too specific.

B Sorry.

A It's fine.
No. It's cool. I'm happy for you.

B Yeh?

A Yeh.
And it was good?

B Really good.

A Better than me?

B It was –

*

B Different. Not better.

A nods.

Tell me about someone you've met.

A   I haven't.

B   In four months.

A   Thanks.

B   I didn't / mean –

A   I'm just tired, OK? With work. My parents.

B   I know.

A   And I'm not photogenic.

B   You are.

A   Not like you.
I did start chatting to this one person but
They sent me a picture of their bumhole.

B   Of –

A   Their bumhole. Yeh.

B   Male or female?

A   Does it matter? A bumhole's a bumhole.

B   That's true.
The great equaliser.

A   . . .

B   We don't have to tell each other this stuff / if you
don't –

A   But then we're not in it together, are we?

B   I guess.

A goes on their phone.

What are you doing?

A Work admin.

B Now?

A . . .

B Is everything OK?

A Fine.

B . . .

B addresses another passenger (P).

Have they said anything about boarding?

P Not yet.

Love your top, by the way.

B Oh. Thank you. It's just second-hand.

P I never find anything that looks that good on me second-hand.

B You must not be looking in the right places.

P Right.

So what are you doing in Berlin, business or pleasure?

B Oh pleasure. Yeh definitely.

A clears their throat.

P The clubs are unreal.
If you go want to get into Berghain, wear black and don't wash your hair.

B OK.

P   And remember not to smile.

B   Good tip.

P   There's actually this night. At Pornsexual
This club.
My ex's boyfriend's friend is DJing. If you want to
come along / I can totally –

B   What kind of night is it?

P   Minimal techno / mainly but –

A   Actually it's our anniversary.

P   Oh.

     Oh. Congrats. How many years?

A   One.

P   Cool.
Well. Have fun.

P turns away.

B goes to put their arm around A.

A   Don't let me interrupt.

B   What?

A   Seriously, keep chatting to your mate.

B   You were on your phone.

A   This is our minibreak. I've never been on holiday
with anyone before.

B   I know.

A   I don't want to go to Berghain.

B   OK.

A   I want to go to galleries and
The Holocaust Memorial. And have a cry.

B   We can / do that too –

A   And have baths. And eat strudel.

B   We will

A   And drink wine. And talk about death and grown-up stuff.

B   We can do both.

      Hey?

A   . . .

B   I'm going to get a green tea, do you want anything?

A   Forgot my keep cup.

B   Oh well.
      Double shot?

A   I'll give you money.

B   If there's only a Starbucks?

A   I don't care, just –

The tannoy sounds.

P   Oh. Boarding's open, guys. See you on there.

A   Too late.

SCENE EIGHT

In A and B's flat. The sound of a shower off.

A   Who is it?

      Who is in the shower?

B   No one.

A No one?

*

B OK, someone but –
    I'm sorry I know this is bad timing / I didn't think –

A I told you.

B What?

A I told you my mum was coming today.

B Your mum

    Shit.
    Shit. That's today?

    B looks at their phone.

A I texted you last night to remind you. I texted you /
    saying –

B Buy loo roll, Mum round at twelve.
    My phone died.
    Shit.

A Why do I have to remind you of our plans again and
    again?

B You don't –

A You're not a free spirit if you don't have a diary, you
    know, you're just a fucking twat.

B It used to be on my iCal.

A You had sex with someone in our flat?

B You were at your parents'.

A Playing brain games with my dad because he's losing
    his words.
    The other day he wanted the TV remote and he just
    kept shouting 'ham and eggs'.

B   Look, I'm sorry, OK, I just / didn't think –

A   Did you have sex in our bed?

B   No.

A   Where?

B   The shower.

And the sofa.

A   I can't believe –
You can't wash that sofa, the covers don't come off.

B   On the upside, the shower self-cleans?

A   . . .

B   You always say you don't mind a bit of mess –

A   Our mess.
You only moved in six weeks ago and / already
you're –

B   We never said it wasn't allowed.

A   I can't believe you had sex with someone on my sofa.

B   Our sofa.

A   I paid for it.

B   It's our flat.

A   I lived here first.

B   But now I do too.

A   Who pays the rent?

B   Don't start that. I pay food and bills.

A   I can't live off pasta and coffee, I'm not a child.

Have you even slept in the last twenty-four hours?

I'm coping with so much and you're out –

What's happening to Dad is like

An earthquake. And I just need one thing, one thing to be stable and normal and that thing is supposed to be you.

Right.

A takes off their shoes.

I want to have a shower. Sort it out.

B Look, I don't have to live here. It was your idea –

A Because you're broke –

B And in case you forgot, it was your idea to open up this relationship, I'm just trying to keep up.

*

A Keep up?
How many people have you slept with since we opened things? In eight months –

B We said we weren't going to talk about / this stuff any more –

A How many?

B Because you don't like / hearing all the –

A You know how many people I've slept with?
Two.

B Not for lack of trying.

A . . .

B Not in a mean way. You're on all the apps.
But you know what, no, you're the one making this about numbers –

A I'm not. I'm just saying for me, this was about connection.

B For me too.

A Who's this then, that you've connected with?
And how did you connect? Orally? Anally?

B We met at Ally's party.

A The house-warming? You went without me?

B You didn't want to go –

A Need I repeat. Ham and eggs.
You could have come with me but no –

B You didn't ask.

A You could ask.

B I don't want to intrude. Sometimes you want me there, sometimes you don't.

A I'm allowed to change my mind.

*

B I would never have come back here, it's just Danny has a partner too, who was at theirs so / we didn't really have much –

A Sorry sorry sorry. Danny? Which is, what? That?

B Yes.

A It has a partner?

B Don't be
It's
Funny. Sort of like a

59

Polyamory chain. Like when you want to sell your house but you have to wait for the other person's buyer to pay up before you can go and / buy it –

A Fuck each other?

I better not know this person.

B You don't. I checked.
Look. Why don't you meet your mum downstairs, take her for coffee. I'll catch you up.

A I don't want to.
I want to meet Danny.

Is that my top?

B I just lent it for the night –

A You lent it to –
I was going to wear that. Now it's all covered in grease and muck.

B OK, Danny's not an urchin.

A Give me your shirt.

B What?

A I want that one.

B You've got loads.

A You used mine.

B I just got dressed.

A So?

B Fine.

*

B takes off their shirt and hands it over.

A And in future don't take / my stuff without asking
and lend it to some random –

Danny (D) enters in trousers and no top, humming.

B Danny.

D Hi.

A Hi.

B Well, this is weird.

D Sorry you must be –

B My partner.

D Of course.
You have a lovely home. That table in the / hall –

A I made it.

D Wow.

Is everything / OK or am I just –

A Yeh, fine. Everything's fine.

D You did know I was here?

B My phone died.

D Ah. So you didn't.

A I did know. In theory. I mean, we are

A Open –

D Oh, thank God. For a minute there, I was like, 'ah' –

D laughs. B laughs.

Worst nightmare.

A   Yeh.

D   Well, anyway, I should probably let you get on with your Saturday.

B   (*to A*) Do you want to go shower then?

A   No I'm good.

B   I think maybe you should. Your mum will be here any second.

D   Your mum? Bad timing (*To B.*) Have you even slept?

B   Um –

D   (*to A*) You know I really recognise you –

                              *

B   Who, me?

D   I meant –

A   Me?

D   Do you know Simon?

A   I don't think so

D   You're an artist, right?

A   No. I make furniture. Well, I run a business that does. Chrysalis Carpentry.

D   Ah. Someone else.

    D starts putting on A's shoes.

A   Those are mine.

D   Oh.

D puts on the correct pair of shoes.

Well. Lovely meeting you.
(*To B.*) Shall I give you my number, maybe we can meet up again?

B We don't really do meeting again.

D Oh –
Well.

D goes in for an embrace goodbye and B awkwardly ducks out of it.

Thanks for last night.

B Yep.

D Bye.

Love this lamp.

D is about to leave, but turns back to A.

You know what, I've remembered. It was on Happn.

A What?

D Happn. That's where I know / you from.

B Happn?

A I don't think so.

D I did, I saw you.

B What's Happn?

D It's this dating app where you can find people you walked past that day. So you never miss a person you fancied. We matched. In Soho.

B You matched / did you –

A   I haven't been there –

D   Soho?

A   Nope.

D   Ever?

A   Not recently.

D   Well that's weird because I definitely Happned with you.

A   I didn't Happn with you.

B   Well, this is really weird.

D   Maybe we should all hang out some time. With my partner. We probably have a lot in common.

A   What, like STDs?

    B laughs.

B   We don't really do hanging out together either.

D   Well, if you ever want to. You know where I am.

*

A   On Happn.

B   OK.

A   Don't talk to my mum, Danny. If you see her.

D   Laters.

B   Yep. Bye. Bye.

    D leaves.

A Christ.

B So what, Happned with you and Danny?

A . . .

B Sorry, couldn't resist.

A Yeh.

B I'm sorry. I shouldn't have –
It was insensitive.
And I need to get better / at checking my –

A Do you want to have sex?

B What? Now?

A Yeh.

B Do we have time, with your mum –

A Five minutes.
Ten maybe.

B Doable.

They kiss.

A It's kind of hot, having sex, when you've just –

B Is it?

A Yeh.

B Fair enough.

They kiss.

B stops.

B You're not thinking about Danny are you?

A What?

No. Why would I be?

B   I don't know.

A   Are you thinking about Danny?

B   No.

A   Well then.

   B goes to start kissing A again.

A   Wait. Why did you ask if I was thinking about Danny? Clearly that means you're thinking about Danny.

B   No it doesn't.

                              *

A   If you want to be with Danny, go and be with Danny.

B   I don't want to.
   Come on, we were going to have sex. It was hot.

A   I'm not in the mood now.

B   Oh come on.
   Don't be like that.
   Now you're in a sulk.

A   I'm not.

B   You are.

                              *

A   I'm not. I'm fine.

B   I don't want to / argue about –

   The door buzzer sounds.

A   And, that'll be my mother.

INTERLUDES

I

— Did you?

— No, but. I don't always.

— I feel bad.

— Don't.

— Do you want to do it yourself and I'll watch?

2

— Is that OK?

— Um –

— Threesomes. Or girl on girl. Boy on boy. Whatever
you like. I just thought it would be hot / to watch
some –

— What just in front of us, while we –

— I can put the laptop on the floor if you like.

3

— Fuck.

— What?

— Fuck. Fuck fuck / fuck fuck fuck fuck fuck fuck

— What? What's wrong?

— What is it?

— Cramp –

4

— Harder.

— Really?

— Harder.

— Are you sure?

— OK.
— Like this?
— Or –

— No. Just take your hand.
— Like this.
— And hit me.
— Hard. In the face.

5

— People make such a big deal out of it.

— . . .

— Why is that so weird?

   . . .

— I don't get it. It's not like you can see them. My feet
    get cold if I take them off. So what?

6

— Coffee or –

— No thanks.

— Tea? I've got mint, green, rooibos, relax or this
    weight loss / stuff my flatmate –

— I should probably just –

— Thanks –

— Oh. OK. Sure.

7

— Shh. (*Laughing.*)

— Shhh. (*Laughing.*)

— You'll wake Tony / (*Laughing.*)

— (*Laughing.*) Tony. This is your unconscious speaking.
    Don't / wake up.

— Shhhhh. (*Laughing.*)

8

— Right is hot, left is cold.

— Thanks.

— Doesn't make sense but
    And my toothbrush is the electric one.

— Is that weird if I. You know.

— I don't know. Is that weird?

— Hottest pic I've seen on this app.

— Haha. Glastonbury babyyyy.

— Your pics are also v beautiful.

— Thank you.

— So what do you do?

— All sorts.

— (*Orgasms.*)

— (*Exhales.*)

— (*Exhales.*)

— Yeh?

— Yeh.

— Open your mouth and I drop it under your tongue.

— And / then I just –

— It kicks in pretty quickly.

— OK and then / we just –

— Relax. Sit back. Enjoy.

— Salt or pepper?

— Salt.

— Fisting or rimming?

— Um.

— Rimming?

— Marmite, yes or no?

— Marmite? A yes or a no.

13

— He's going to make me cum. Do you want him to make me cum?

— Yeh.

— Touch her at the same time.

— I am.

— Touch her. And you touch him. At the same time. Yes. I want us all to cum at the same time. OK? Ready? Are you ready? I'm close. I'm getting close. Are you close? Are you? I'm going to. I'm going to. I'm going to. I'm going to.

SCENE NINE

In a therapist's room. There are three chairs. The therapist (T) sits on one. A and B sit on the others.

A So just I, not you?

T That's right.

A As in, I feel exhausted by your shit. Not you exhaust me with your shit?

T There is still a you in 'your shit' strictly speaking / but –

71

A It's a your.

T Just 'I' statements.

A I feel exhausted by the shit?

T Perfect.

A I feel
Tired?
I feel stressed. I never expected to be a company
director, I just did woodwork.

I guess I feel like I'm a sell-out somehow?
But I spent most of my twenties dicking around, now
I want to make something.

And with my dad. It's weird. I know I'm losing him.
But there's these moments of –

Redoing his buttons when he's done them up wrong or
Teaching him words again.

It's like, I'm the parent now, and he's the child. And
it's kind of
Magic. In some ways we're closer than ever.

But it does make you feel kind of –

Disconnected, you know? Like you've joined this new
club and not everyone's in it. The 'sick parents' club.
I want to shake everyone else and be like, stop being
so fucking

Petty.

I don't know. Maybe I'd be better off single. I know I
can be a dick.

T Let's try and keep this as a non-judgemental space.
No one is a dick here.

A Right.

T   Thank you.

(*To B.*) Now, if you would like to / start –

B   Yup. So I relate back, but don't comment?

T   That's right.

B   By relate do you mean / I –

A   Just do what it says on the paper.

B   I am.

(*To A.*) OK, you feel stressed at work. Chrysalis exploded the same time I quit, so –

(*To T.*) I used to work in branding for / a big company –

A   Could you just focus on me please? For a second. That's the point of the exercise.

B   You own a company. That's a lot of pressure. Suddenly you're beholden to other people. You're losing a parent, which is awful. I can't imagine what it must be like to –

A   I –

B   What?

A   See? You said I. This is meant to be about me and you still / manage to –

B   I didn't mean
    I didn't mean 'I' like me, I meant –

A   You don't understand.

B   I don't pretend to.

T   I sense a lot of anger between you.

73

A   / I'm not angry

B   I'm not angry, I'm just hurt –

T   That's interesting. (*To B.*) You feel hurt.

B   I just

I mean, you meet a person. You mould your life around them, and they keep changing the goalposts.

T   Which goalposts?

B   I try to get it right with your dad.
I tried the open relationship.

A   Oh, you tried.

B   See what I mean? I'd do anything to make you happy / and you just –

A   Maybe that's the problem. I don't want someone to make me happy, I want someone to be themselves.

B   You think that's what you want but. You like calling the shots, that's why you picked me, I'm floppy.

A   That's not why I picked you. I picked you because you were kind. And funny. And weird –
Now it's like I don't recognise you.

B   Whose fault is that?

A switch point occurs but A stops it.

A   No. Stop. Stop blaming other people. (*To T.*) Do you see this? (*To B.*) You are so full of shit. You're doing exactly what you want, what you never did as a teenager, in your suburban bubble. I'm just a vehicle for / you to explore –

B   A vehicle? Fuck off.

T   I'd like us to refrain from using denigrating language if we can.

74

B Denigrating?

A It means nasty.

B . . .

T I'm interested in what you said about things changing. Managing expectations is a big part of a relationship. What do you think you expected when you met?

A Reliability.

B Excitement.

T Therein lies 'the rub'.

What was the open relationship about? Testing those things? You should know, tests don't work, except in science. And love is not a science, hm?
Do you feel the two are compatible? 'Reliability'? 'Excitement'?

B That's a lot of – (*Makes a gesture to indicate quote marks.*)

T Maybe that's because it's all hypothetical. You.

This.

Another switch point occurs but A and B resist it.

The future.

A relationship is never a conclusion. They say, love is a verb. Because no one will love us unconditionally. Not even our parents. And nothing in life stays the same.

A Except death and taxes.

B And tax evasion.

(*To T.*) Starbucks is our in-joke.

A   We're aware it's very sad.

B takes A's hand.

B   I'm sorry I don't always get it right with your Dad.
    I'll try harder.

A   Just be there. That's enough.

T   Well.
    As we close I wonder if I could show you something
    I share with couples when we talk about seeing things
    differently. It's just a picture. Bit silly I know, but –

*T gets out a picture. It has a man on one side and a
woman on another and a squiggle in the middle of
them. To the man it looks like an M, to the woman it
looks like a W.*

B   Bit gendered.

A   What?

B   A man seeing an M and a woman seeing a W.

T   Fair point.

A   It's just a squiggle.

B   No it's not. It's a man seeing an M / and a woman –

A   I just see a squiggle. In the middle. Like a zigzag.

B   It's clearly a man and a woman, you can see her little
    triangle skirt.

A   But that's not the point. It's about perspectives.

B   I understand what it is. I don't need it explaining to
    me / I'm just saying it's a bit binary.

A   OK, sorry.
    It's not binary.
    Why does it matter?

B   It matters to me.

A   Why?

B   It just does.

T   I take your point. Perhaps it's time I
    Re-jigged the image a bit.

    Let's try and leave things on a positive note, shall we?
    Perhaps you could both say one thing you're grateful
    for in the relationship?

A   Grateful?

T   Yes. Anything you like.

A   You go first then.

B   No, please, you.

SCENE TEN

*In a hospital. A's father lies unconscious in a bed in
between A and B.*

B   I didn't know Alzheimer's could cause a stroke.

A   It wasn't the Alzheimer's. The stroke was just a
    stroke.

B   God.

    Love, I am so sorry.

    B comes towards A.

A moves backwards slightly.
B stops.

Where's everyone else?

A Getting some sleep. My sister's down the pub.

B Classic Janet.

A I brought your phone. Found it when I kept trying to call you.

B Sorry. Left it behind. Lucky I met Ally for lunch so you could reach me.

Hey –

B comes towards A again.

A You can sit.

B Is everything OK?
I mean, obviously it's not OK / but –

A Everything's fine.

B Good.
Well –

A Except that you're a fucking lying fucking cunt.

B What?

A We said we'd stopped.

B Stopped?

A After we talked things through
These last six months were
Like a burst of colour. I thought, God we've found it.
This is how it's supposed to feel.

B What are you talking about?

A On your phone your inbox was weirdly empty? Like stuff had been deleted? Then I checked your texts to Ally. You forgot to delete those.
I bet a lot of people do that.

A reads from B's phone.

'I know it's awful. But the nipple ring oh my God. And being with a nineteen-year-old. Am I a bad person?'

B . . .

A The answer Ally was looking for was yes.

Take your time I've got all evening

B You went through my phone?

A What?

B You checked my messages?

A I checked them because when I check them I find shit like this.

B One time –

A . . .

B Look –

A What? Go on.

B Can we go outside / please.

A No.

B Please. We can't do this here.

A If my dad dies while I'm outside hearing about you fucking someone with a nipple ring, I will really never forgive you.

B Look. I am so sorry. I can't believe this is happening now but –
I was going to tell you.

A When? At the funeral?
Or after, when I'm in a really good mood?

B I didn't know this was going to happen now / did I?

A So what, it took this to make you actually give a shit about me?

B It was one stupid mistake.

A Who is this person? The nineteen-year-old?

B Jay.

A Jay.

B We met on my course.

Well, Jay studies Fine Art not History of Art / but still –

A I don't care what Jay studies, I really don't.

B We met in the bar.

A The student bar?
Which you go to? When I'm working late or with the geriatrics, is that right?

B Just for the odd drink.

A Nice.

Go on.

B That weekend when you went to the trade show in
Manchester, we all got drunk.
Some people were high. I'd just finished my
dissertation. We ended up bar-hopping in New Cross.
I was off my head. Went to the toilet and my face in
the mirror was –

                              *

Different. Vibrating almost.

A And –

B Um
We ended up in a hotel.

A Kinky.

B It was a Marriott.

A . . .

B It was so stupid. It just felt right, in that moment.

A The first time we had sex was in a hotel, do you
remember?

B Ally's wedding.

A What is Ally doing bar-hopping? Ally's married.

B Ally's never cheated.

A Oh great. Let's celebrate, where's the fucking piñata.
So why a hotel?

B Well, Jay lives in a squat, so –

A Oh my God you really are having a mid-life crisis.

B Well. Not quite mid-life, but –

A And this Jay knew, that you lived with me?

B shakes their head.

A Right.

B That's how I knew this wasn't OK, I could tell myself
that it was, but I knew it wasn't because when we
were doing the open relationship thing, we always
said –

  It was a huge mistake. A stumble. I want to be with
  you, not anyone else.

A And since then?

B We haven't spoken. Haven't seen each other.

A Right.

B Except –

A Great.

B Except. I got high that weekend you were on the tech
course and I did –
We did text then.

A Text?

B It was more of a

  Sext.

A A sext?

B I'm sorry. I don't know / what else to –

A Were there pictures?

B Pictures?

A As part of the sexts?

B Yes.

A Oh?

B I

Sent a picture.

A You sent a picture.

B Yes.

A Of?

B Of –

A Everything?

B Most
Things.

A From what angle? Crotch shot? Pouting from above?

B Just, a picture of me with no clothes on.

A I guessed that.

You know cheating has a certain frisson. At least it's.
I don't know
Brave. Kind of a brave thing you do to cope with
boredom. Make you feel alive.
And maybe you were angry with me / or we were
having a bad week –

B I honestly wasn't. You didn't do anything.

A But sexting. What are you, a teenager?
Even when teenagers do that, everyone thinks they're
fucking thick.

B Look I'm sorry. It was a mistake. I'm so ashamed.
I love you.
I want to marry you.

A You want to marry me? You want to fucking marry
me? You'd want to marry a fucking carrot if it told
you it loved you enough.

Send me the sext.

B What?

A Send it to me. I want to see it.

B I don't know if I've still got it.

A I think you know.

B gets out their phone.

A Turn you on, does it?

B I don't know.
I guess I just thought I looked good.

A Send it to me.

B I don't think you're meant to text / in a hospital.

A Send it.

B looks at their phone.

B sends the sext.
A looks at their phone.

A Bit grainy.
But you look good.

B Please. I beg you / just let me –

A Seriously, you haven't looked that good in ages. You must have put on weight.
Even better on my grown-up smartphone, look.
Much bigger.

Shame you don't have Whatsapp. On your edgy little retro phone.

A types on their own phone.

B   What?

A   It's a great way of connecting people. I can have
     conversations with twenty of my friends at once.
     Send them all pictures.
     Where's that big group chat we made for Pride last
     year?

     Here we go.
     'Proud. Two men emoji. Two women emoji.
     Aubergine emoji'. What fun we had –

B   What are you –

A   It's as simple as clickety-click. Forward photos. Send.

B   Are you

     Are you joking?

A   Would it be funny if I was?

B   Please don't do this.

A   I'll do what the fuck I want.

B   Please.
     Please.
     Please –

A   What about Ally's friends? There's a thread on here
     somewhere.

B   No –

A   Your family maybe?

B   Please. I beg you –

A   Scare the living daylights out of their Tory souls.

B   Come on.

A   You're my partner aren't you? If I'm sharing you then
     let's really fucking share you. Let's share until there's

millions of you everywhere, is that what you want, so you can be with everyone all the time? Is that the point?

Do I even matter? Does anyone matter to you?

*

To anyone?

B Did you send it?

A You don't care about me.

B Did you?

A You don't care.

Go find someone else.

The door opens and a Nurse (N) walks in.

N Sorry. Just here to do bloods.

A I'm going to the pub to take over from Janet. You should come. Might be some teenagers you can drag to the Premier Inn.

A leaves.

B looks at their phone.

N (*to B*) No phones on the wards, love, I'm sorry.

B Sorry.

N You a relative?

B No.

N Just here with your partner?

B No. I'm no one special.

*

I'm no one.

SCENE ELEVEN

At a funeral. A is alone onstage. They have just spilt their drink.

A Fuck.

They try to clear it up.

B enters.

B What happened?

A Nothing.

B Do you need a –

A I'm fine.

B I could go and / get some –

A I said I'm fine. Just leave it.

B OK.

Beautiful service.

A . . .

B Thank you for inviting me.

A My parents always loved you.

Good knows why.

A stops cleaning up.

B   Been a long time. Since number twelve.

The allotments.
You know they're knocking them down? Investors
building flats. Little concrete pods on top of Alan's
tomato plants.

B offers the plate to A.

Canapé?
Bit stale but –

A shakes their head.

Janet read well.

A   Managed to stay sober.

B   Don't speak too soon. Saw her minesweeping by the
quiche lorraine. She tried to act casual but those
glasses of sherry can't all be hers.

Lovely flowers.

Look, I'm sorry. I should have visited. I know / there
was –

A   Do you want to know something funny?

B   Yes please.

A   It's quite dark.

B   Go for it.

A   OK.

When we were in the hospice, about six months after
the stroke, I was in Dad's room, watching what was
left of him breathing through this machine.

So weird, it looked like him, but it wasn't. Just a shell.

And this person comes in to visit.

I thought it must be an old work colleague.

And this stranger sits there, crying and everything, and says, we were having an affair.

B What?

A Yep.

Showed me their messages.

It had been going on eight years.

B Eight?

A And then, last week, Janet and I were at the house sorting through papers.

Mum was at yoga. And the doorbell goes and another person –

B No.

A A different person comes in and says, oh yes, did you not know? I was seeing your Dad a few years back.

Heard he was dead through social media. Just turned up.

My dad.

B How did he have time?

A As long as they keep replacing hips.

The worse thing is, I asked my Mum about it, trying to be all sensitive, and she just shrugged and said, you do what works for you.

They were both full of shit.

I hate him.

B   No you don't.

A   I do. I hate him for lying.

B   It's just a –

Generational thing. They find it hard to talk about this stuff.

A   But why lie? It's me. I don't care what he did ,I just care that it makes me feel like I didn't even matter enough for him to want to know me. Properly.

And I know it's stupid and I feel ashamed saying it but I guess some part of me used to look at my parents and think –

It can happen. They love each other that much. And they love me. And maybe one day, someone will look at me and think

And I can't even shout at him. We can't even fight about it. He's just gone. I hate that thought. The bit inside, the bit you loved, it just goes out like a light and then –

Just another body.

People say they're meant to stay with you after they die but I can't feel him. He's not there anymore. He's gone. And I don't want it to be over.

B   Hey.

A   I don't want him to be gone. There are still things we need to say.

B   I know.

A   I have things to say.

B   Hey. Can I?

B hugs A.

A   I looked at the pictures of him in there.

      He looks so like me.

A   And I thought. Who the fuck is that?

      I don't know who I'm supposed to mourn for.

B   I guess –

      Mourn for the person you loved?

*

A   Sorry.

B   No.

      Good to know you have feelings.
      Other than blind rage.

A   Mostly that.

B   Yeh.

A   How are you?

B   Fine.
      Fine.

A   You went away?

B   Travelling. After my course. Thought I'd clear my
      head. So –
      Brazil.

A   Carnival?

B   Yeh.

A   Nice.
      What's next?

B Not sure.
I'd quite like to live abroad for a bit. It's all up in the air.

How's Chrysalis?

A Good.
Stocked on Amazon now.

B Sorry for your loss.

A They're actually great to work with.
Fuckers.

B You're doing so well.

A Mm.

Are you seeing anyone?

B Are you sure you want to / talk about –

A Go on. Rip the plaster off.

B I've been seeing a fair bit of Sam.

A Sam as in. Your ex?

B nods.

A Ah.

Nine years. Long time.

B Maybe we needed some time apart you know, to –

I feel weird talking to you about this.

A No, I want to.

B We're taking things slow. Getting to know each other again.

Are you with anyone?

A A few people. No one I could bring to this.

Do you think Sam is your person?

B Well, there's not one person for any of us is there? That was probably the one thing we agreed on.

A But what if you're my person and Sam's your person? Do you think that can happen?

B I don't know.

A Or what if we got it wrong. Do you think we'll realise in time?

B In time for –

A Alzheimer's?
The world ending?
Marriage and kids?

B Hopefully not in that order.

A Look, I know I shouldn't say this but I don't want to wait another ten years to bump into you because then you'll have some snotty kid and I'll be ravaged by work and trauma / or maybe I'll be dead –

B You won't.

A But please –

Stay. Please. Just stay the night with me.

B Where?

A Anywhere. A B&B.
Your car? Have you got your car with you?

B Yes.

A   Drop me home in the morning.

B checks their phone.

B   I should go.

A   Really?

B   Sam.

A   Yeh but

One last time.

It'll be fun.

I'll agree with everything you say. I'll be nice.

B   I don't think it's a good idea. You've got your family.
You need to mourn.

A   I think I'll be doing that forever.
I mean I know I will, but
You won't be here forever. We won't have these

Opportunities.

B   Having an opportunity doesn't mean you should
take it.

A   Maybe.

B   Last time this happened look how we ended up. In a
room called Camel's Hump.

A   I don't regret it.

B   I don't either but I don't think it would be good.
Now. You know –

A   Maybe it would be the best kind of bad.

B   You sound like a trashy novel.

A   I don't care. I'll do whatever it takes.
I'll go full chick lit.